This book belongs to:

_____

From:

_____

MARIGOLD PRESS BOOKS

A division of International School of Story
Savannah, Georgia

ISBN: 978-1-942923-61-9 (paperback)
978-1-942923-62-6 (hardback)

Copyright © 2023 Dr. Kia Harren

Cover Design by Skye McLeod
Typesetting Design & Illustrations by Ashlyn Rizk
Fonts licensed for use.

See What I See!

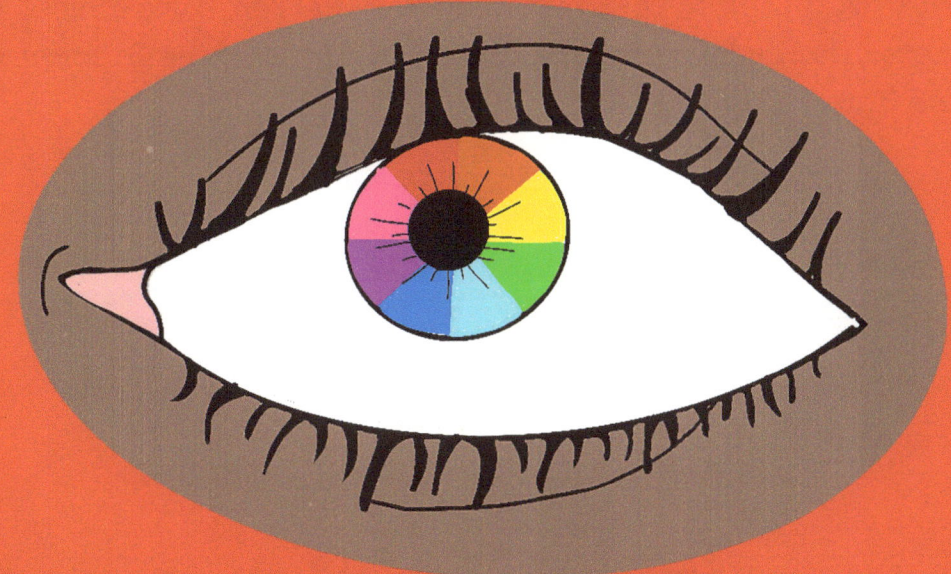

By Dr. Kia Harren

A Tribute to my Children and Grandchildren:

CHILDREN – Shanequia Foster, Heaven Brunson, Theodore J. Brunson Jr., Zaria Fontaine, Kyle Harren, and Brody Harren.

GRANDCHILDREN – Ely Harren, Mallory Harren, Parker Seras, Carter Foster, Rowan Harren, John Foster, Taylor Fontaine Jr., Hope Foster, and Baby Fontaine.

Remember, you can . . . so keep on reading!

A Special Tribute:

To my late husband, Theodore J. Brunson Sr., who supported me as I began this project journey.

An Extra Special Tribute:

To my parents, Pastor Lawrence A. Reeves Jr. and the late Beanie E. Reeves. Thank you for being positive role models and always being in my corner. Parents like you are truly a blessing.

Dedication:

I dedicate this book to my best friend, my love, my partner, my husband...

David C. Harren

Thank you so much for supporting me as I completed this project journey that began three years ago.

I thank God for your presence daily!

2

I see two

blue

squares!

3

I see three

orange triangles!

I see
5
five

yellow
hexagons!

I see 6 six brown ovals!

7
I see seven

black diamonds!

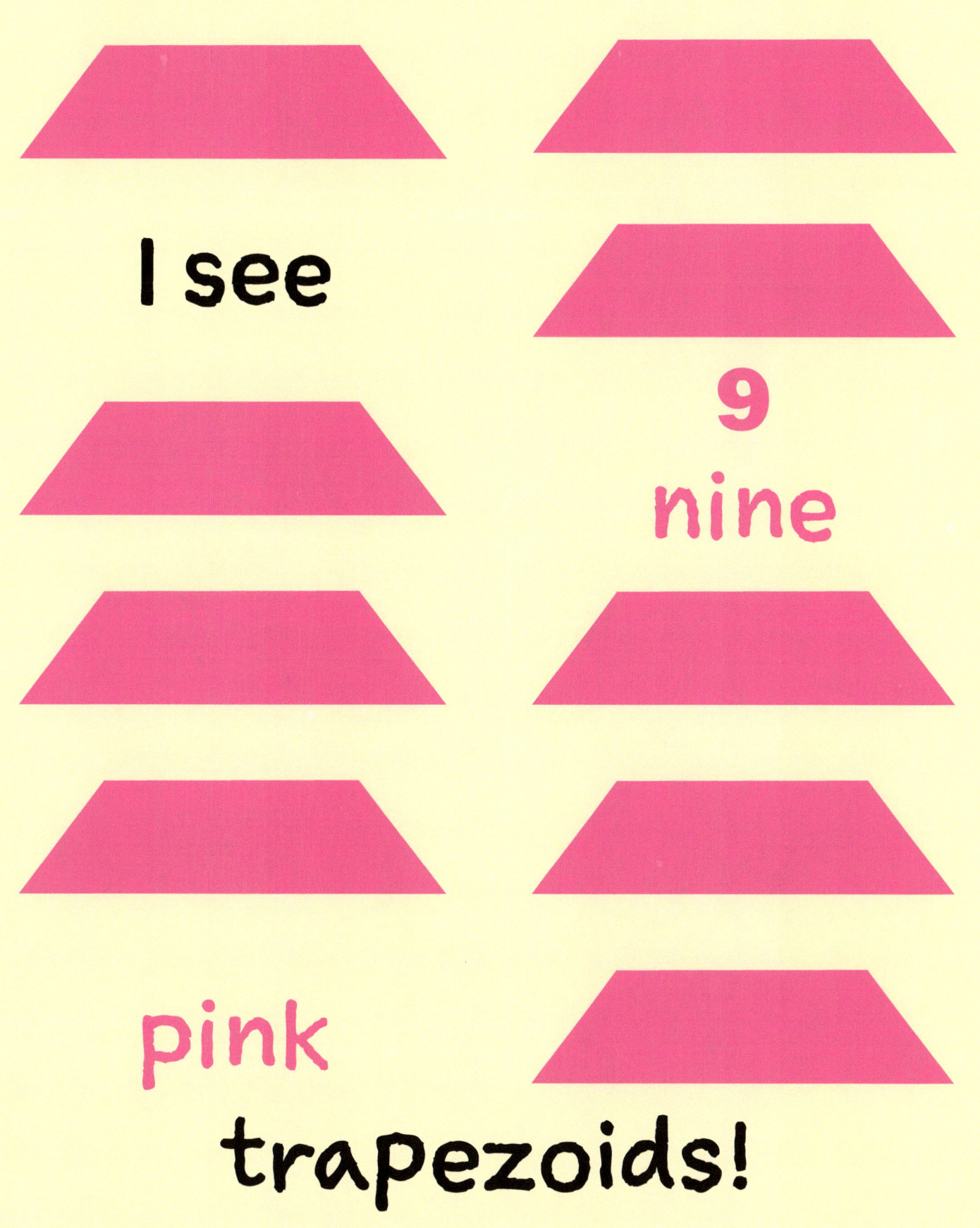

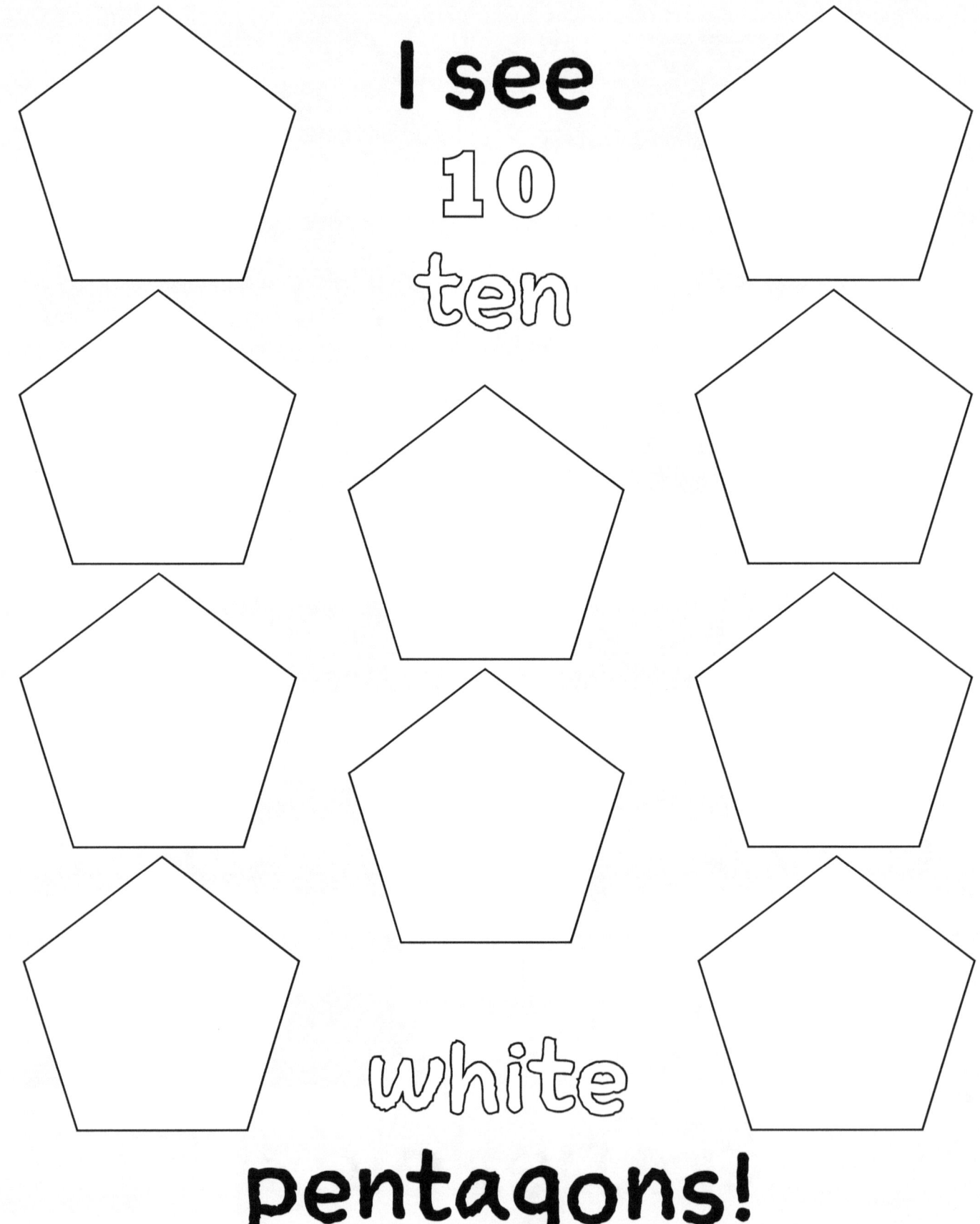

Dr. Harren's Motto

"I am somebody.
I am successful.
I am a leader.
Failure is not an option."

The Author's Journey
Dr. Kia Harren

November 11, 1975, Kia Monique Reeves was born at Grady Hospital in Atlanta, Georgia. She was only daughter of Pastor Lawrence and Beanie Reeves. Kia grew up in Atlanta along with her three brothers, Lawrence III, Corey, and James.

In the early grades, Kia was a below average to average learner. By the time she reached high school, she studied hard and earned the honor of Salutatorian of her 1993 graduating class.

In May 1997, Kia earned her BS in Education. Later that year in November, she began her teaching career with the Liberty County School System. In 2003, she earned her Masters Degree in Instructional Supervision. In 2006, she earned a Specialist Degree in Educational Leadership and was bestowed the honor of Teacher of the Year for Waldo Pafford Elementary School in Hinesville, Georgia. Kia culminated her education in 2016, by obtaining her Doctoral Degree in Educational Leadership.

In the midst of her education, Kia met and married Theodore Brunson in 1996, changing her name from Ms. Kia Reeves to Mrs. Kia Brunson, then Dr. Kia Brunson. Theodore and Kia lived in Hinesville and then Ludowici, Georgia, where they successfully raised four children.

After 24 years of marriage, in 2021, Mr. Brunson passed away. In 2022, Dr. Kia Brunson met and married David Harren, which changed her name once again, to Dr. Kia Harren.